THE
DROWNING HOUSE

THE
DROWNING HOUSE

John Sibley Williams

ELIXIR PRESS
DENVER, COLORADO

Book design by Steven Seighman
Cover art: *Keeper of the Flame*, Daniel Mark Cassity

Library of Congress Cataloging-in-Publication Data

Names: Williams, John Sibley, author.
Title: The drowning house / John Sibley Williams.
Description: First edition. | Denver, Colorado : Elixir Press, 2021. |
Summary: "Winner of the Elixir Press 21st Annual Poetry Award"--
Provided by publisher.
Identifiers: LCCN 2021042511 | ISBN 9781932418781 (paperback)
Subjects: LCGFT: Poetry.
Classification: LCC PS3623.I55813 D76 2021 | DDC 811/.6--dc23
LC record available at https://lccn.loc.gov/2021042511

ISBN: 978-1-932-41878-1

First edition: 2022

10   9   8   7   6   5   4   3   2   1

CONTENTS

• Summon •

ACKNOWLEDGEMENTS

The Adirondack Review: Prometheus // Trayvon Martin

American Literary Review: In the beginning the bodies were too soft

Balkan Press: Rosa Parks // Banksy (Winner of the Carl Sennehen Poetry Prize)

Bennington Review: Mask

The Best American Poetry 2021 anthology: The Dead Just Need to be Seen. Not Forgiven. (reprint)

Blackbird: Incarnate and The Moon is Two Half-Moons Joined Together

Boulevard: Picture Day

Briar Cliff Review: Emmett Till // Edward Hopper

Bryant Literary Review: Charcoal Nude

The Comstock Review: Assimilation

COG: Incendiary Device, Dissolve, and The Sacred (Winner of the *COG* Poetry Award)

Colorado Review: Bloom

Connecticut River Review: Counterglow

Construction: It's Not Corpses We Burn on Pyres Anymore (Finalist for the *Construction* Poetry Prize)

Crab Creek Review: What I Tell Them (Finalist for *Crab Creek* Poetry Prize)

DIALOGIST: Uncoordinated Efforts and Jean-Michel Basquiat // Harriet Tubman

EX/POST: Conquistador

The Florida Review: Invasive

The Fourth River: Postscript for a Flyover Country

Free Verse: A Journal of Contemporary Poetry & Poetics: The Last Sunset

Green Mountains Review: Figurehead

Grey Sparrow Journal: That is Really Just Rope

Hotel Amerika: Prototype

Jet Fuel Review: I Tend to See Love as an Absence of Context

JuxtaProse: Summon

The Madison Review: Regardless, there will be bodies and Everything here is beautiful (Winner of the Phyllis Smart-Young Prize)

The Museum of Americana: Nikola Tesla // Malala Yousafzai and César Estrada Chávez // Robert Frost

New American Writing: Harps strung with gut still make music after 2,000 years

New Statesman: Sisyphus // Roger Ailes

Ninth Letter: The Drowning House and Dark Tourist (Winner of the *Ninth Letter* Award for Poetry)

North Dakota Review: The wolves have done their worst

Poetry Super Highway: Second Generation (Selected as Poem of the Week)

Porter House Review: A Poem in Which Everyone Survives Until Dawn, Separations, and Pantomime (Finalist for the *Porter House Review* Editor's Prize)

RHINO: Self-Portrait as Lacuna

Ruminate: I too take shelter in the body and Encroachment (Winner of the Janet B. McCabe Poetry Prize)

Santa Fe Literary Review: Internment

Sepia Journal: Self-Portrait of Public Crucifixion

Smartish Pace: Meadowslash

South Dakota Quarterly: Americanisms

Southern Indiana Review: The Dead Just Need to be Seen. Not Forgiven. (Finalist for the Mary C. Mohr Awards)

Subnivean: First Ocean

Sycamore Review: My American Ghost (Winner of the Wabash Prize in Poetry)

TriQuarterly: Our Daily Breads

Valparaiso Poetry Review: Self-Portrait with Mojave

Verse Daily: Picture Day (reprint)

Willow Springs: Seed and My Heart is in the Mouth of Another Heart

The Worcester Review: On Being Told: *To Tear It All Down is To Rebuild*

The Writing Salon: Armistice (Winner of the Jane Underwood Poetry Prize)

The following poems were also included in the chapbook *Summon*, winner of the 2019 JuxtaProse Chapbook Contest: Dissolve, Pantomime, Bloom, Dark Tourist, The Dead Just Need to be Seen. Not Forgiven., Incendiary Device, Separations, The Drowning House, Internment, Everything here is beautiful, Summon, The Sacred, My Heart is in the Mouth of Another Heart, and My American Ghost.

IN THE BEGINNING THE BODIES WERE TOO SOFT

& the land too hard. Or the other way around.
But nothing interred, stayed, left a place tender
enough to visit armed with flowers, tiny animal
bones strung together into trinkets, the already
waning nostalgias meant to capture the entirety
of a life. & of a life, the living said only what
needed saying. All things being equal, turns out
all things are pretty much equal. Imagine it: all
the might it takes to forget & be okay with that
forgetting. To tear wildly into, open up, plant,
& know the animals not repulsed by death will
come for the rest. They came for the rest as one
comes to dinner, still, not invited exactly, more
called by the smell of it, that honeyed smell,
stripping ruin of its ruin, savoring it, putting to
good use the boys the earth spit back up. Earth
still spits, I'm told by the people stripped of all
but a few arid acres, gifted as a sort of apology,
amends. They tell me the land is still too hard
or too soft & the bodies that can't enter it.

—*for Abigail Chabitnoy*

MY AMERICAN GHOST

PANTOMIME

—for Jamaal May

Outside sheets are pulling
back together into bodies.

The wind confuses sway
with dance, asks the dresses

there's no one left to wear
for one more go before

the music ends. We wait
for the well out back to

illuminate its drowned coins,
all the gods overrun by prayers

to choose just this one to answer.
We beat the rain from hanging

undershirts & sing like nothing
the sky can do can rust the birds

from our mouths. We promise
our children the world

is forever, that this time
the wolves won't show.

The fields are smoke
& through the smoke

figures materialize.
Deer that might be

mothers or sisters, gutshot,
looking for a slice of shadow

to die in. So many hanging trees
we confuse with men.

EMMETT TILL // EDWARD HOPPER

In your mouth, a thousand unpainted churches—
steeples snapped off like baby teeth in an apple,

rusted bells trying so hard to ring. Ringing.
Crows along your restless edges, where

clapboard meets sky. & storm. The sky is
always storming. Skin can be its own

broken republic. Everywhere,
overgrown rail tracks and a few white people

who don't know what to say to each other.
Not anymore. Truth is married to the surface

of things. The surface is a lighthouse
overlooking wreck after wreck. No ships

here anymore. Nothing left to cradle & swing
safely into harbor. All sorts of things swing.

All sorts of women sit on the knife's edge
of a bed, half-naked, staring out a half-

naked window. All sorts of men are tossed
over bridges after whistling a little tune.

Come back, crows. Bells. Edges. In you,
let the night see its face.

THE DEAD JUST NEED TO BE SEEN. NOT FORGIVEN.

That old man in the photo our family never talks about,
known best for tracking runaway slaves; tonight

we drag him from the basement up these loose
wood stairs & set out a plate of salted cabbage & rabbit—

so long since I've asked why the empty chair at our table.
With all the warmth a body has to give, we give up on

measuring the darkness between men. Dust & dusk enter
& are wiped from the room. The names we call each other

linger luminous & savage. Still. That tree I used to hang
tires from holds tight its dead centuries. The light

swinging from its branches we call rope-like,
which implies there's no longer rope. Tonight, we'll wash

the burnt-out stars from his hair, all the crumbs from his beard.
The misfired bullet of his voice we let burn as it must.

REGARDLESS, THERE WILL BE BODIES

dragged for miles behind rusty pick-ups filled with boys
daring the night to stop them.

Sparrows downed by stones: & the stones. Windows
shot out: air rifle, & a kitchen floor

gone sharp underfoot. Praise be the uncrossable lines,
so easily crossed:

the knifework it takes to open a small animal, a lawn cross
burning bright.

Because there is no other ending, how we rush,
others first, toward oblivion.

Praise be the mass silence before, after, & during.
That it's okay

to do what we do as long as everyone
is there to witness.

—after James Byrd Jr.

AMERICANISMS

How around the abandoned edges

just past those red painted boards
we may someday nail together
into a barn but before you get to
that evergreen-scented wildness
as children we never dared enter
without weapons & our fathers

a whole town strewn with half-lit
neon bars & matching houses rises
from dusk into a deeper darkness.

How ever since the factory fell

into smokeless silence, the men
have brought their rough & raging gods
home to tend to like another man's child.
& how we love them all the more for it.

Mineral-rich runoff from last month's
snows work its way down to us as spit
from a boy's burning cheek. Nobody

told us the difference between skins
until ours lost some of its privilege.
Now it's as if we're hoping disharmony
unifies us. & maybe it can. Everyone

counting their breaths like the disquiet
between thunderclap & lightning strike.
Everyone walking bitterly on their mouths.

Perhaps the darkness of the house can
hold it all together. An unarmed sky heavy
with promises cracks open into another
storm. The bars are all 24-7 now. How
when we say *the thing that's wrong with*

this country, the *forgive me* is implied.

ENCROACHMENT

Yes, any evening field, where deer thank the wolves
for diverting a hunter's love; whatever it means to be
lesser prey—we'll take it. Yes,

×

to keep the wild in its place
or have something to hand a son
harder than a woman's

body—also

the dug-under barbed wire fencing
meant to shelter gentler animals wholly
inadequate, now, the way things are now; yes

×

—but it's more than hunger;
that light that never leaves even after the eating

×

arouses or—a kind of progress—desensitizes, less
out of moral weakness than the *more more please
more* of living this long, which demands a degree

of distance: physical & emotional. *Orison*

is an archaic word for prayer. Prayer is an archaic word
for loving at least one thing more than myself. I refuse

   to love equally

the bullet & its target. That we are all targets; some,
thankfully, lord, not today.

PROMETHEUS // TRAYVON MARTIN

Not always intentional, this hauling
fire down from the heavens, humanizing

the grand machinery of witness. Sometimes
the Titan deep within a hungry young man

propels him out into streets owned by
ferocious gods, heavied by a handful

of sweetness, expecting nothing more
than night and the knowledge that night

only lasts so long. Who knew eagles
could feast forever? That gods don't share

their fire freely? Goddamn this ever-
regenerating liver, this body lashed

to rock lashed by sea imprisoned in
its own tender enormity. Before dissolving

into myth, newsprint, statistic, sometimes
a body wears the world like this: brutally

bright: innocent: that bit of starshine shot through
constant night. In the flame he's handed us, unwittingly,

an ugly gratitude. A *thank you* without reply. A mother
without a son. Eagle and skin. His skin, still a heresy.

SELF-PORTRAIT WITH MOJAVE

White as a picked apart cattle skull,
clean & sober as its dismantling,

our eyes grown accustomed to seeing
ghosts seek out other kinds of horror.

Enormous horse hides fill the walls.
A Winchester rides high over pictures

of a blacked & whited history. The people
who've called this place home longer

than we've been Americans squat outside
a gas station sipping at bottles we gave

them in compensation, in apology.
As kids we'd drag the shed part of snakes

home to decorate a stone mantle
that never needed to know fire.

How we'd light it anyway
to let the land know

we're not going anywhere.
How we'd let the water cupped

in our hands escape back to the basin
& think it thirst.

INTERNMENT

—for Vanessa Angélica Villarreal

Draw a line   from the river's   throat down

      to where it empties

bloodlessly   into a larger   body, assimilating

           salt & gull & all the narratives

of the West. Unspeak   your source language
                         of mountain

& salmon, frost, all 1,243 miles it took   to reach open sea.

        Whatever you were promised   waited

here has been rescinded; like the light   at the end of all tunnels.

            This country goes

weak at the knees at the thought of you,   how you nourish
   the earth

      & give the animals something to drink.

      Still the animals are thirsty.

          This new sky   still the same
sterile   white   sheet you might wrap around a child

separated from her parents.

WHAT I TELL THEM

In the shallows a boy
    holds another boy's head

under until the thrashing
    calms to a loving

obedience. In this version
    he unlocks his fist-

ful of dark hair before
    the breathing stops

& the whole wooded walk
    home they laugh at

how fingers learn to tolerate
    their matches. In time

trust the burning. That thing
    they feared most

not handed down another
    generation. Blackness

& everything it carries.
    In the version

I repeat to my children
    evenings over

their well-built cribs meant

to withstand my weight

& my father's & his
    both boys shake

off the shadows the world
    has splayed for them.

Even if it means belt & bruise,
    they'll return to the river together.

Even if I have to add some talking animals
    to make it sound true.

ON BEING TOLD: *TO TEAR IT ALL DOWN IS TO REBUILD*

slowly I let the story spill
    through my fingers, not so
different than the rice grandma
    washes ten thousand times

before steaming off the rest
    of our blood or the water
we imagine heaving every morning
    up from that dried-out well

the old folks say old folks once
    drowned their pregnant
cats in to keep this tiny fenceless
    sliver of the world in check

this time it's the uncle whose hands softly
    rummaged through our childhoods
like yard sale knickknacks craning over his
    rabbit & cabbage talking without

end about the end of a republic,
    the knife pressed to the white
man's jugular, the obsolete
    uses of rope, how cottonwood

limbs just aren't the same anymore &, abandoned,
    the god within
the overgrown boarded up church
    is calling it quits:

as in the hollow silo out back must burn

us into forgiveness,
as in it's the blood in the rice that
   gives it flavor; he says

now we must rebuild love,
   brick-by-brick, body-by-another's-
broken-body; this glorious cathedral
   no one, nobody, enters without

someone else's sacrifice

OUR DAILY BREADS

As if she waded through brown rivers [ ] clawed
mountains down to valleys expecting something [ ]

potable, a rivulet of mother tears or lake [ ] of children's,
as if she abandoned wide-open cage [ ] for cage, swollen

belly for another kind of [ ] hunger, picked up the only
job that didn't ask [ ] questions & argued with her god

every night over the meaning of [ ] night, the town over-
priced to keep the dollars [ ] on this side of a border

that doesn't look like much [ ] of a border, more intersect
where field meets matching field, where three children [ ]

are already learning a language they pray [ ] to use some-
day to speak with a mother whose [ ] face vagues from

memory [ ] the harder [ ] they try to wear it [ ]
over their own [ ] [ ] [ ] [ ] [ ] [ ]

ROSA PARKS // BANKSY

Incendiary still, although the flowers
in truth were meant for your mother

whose life, in the way of lives, was
thrashing about inside while nothing

in her eyes recognized your face. Still,
the same impact as a Molotov cocktail.

The same discolored water & burning
color. Thirsting roots contrasted against

a stagnant sky. Is it a prayer, this gesture,
this song? Someone tells you to stand.

Someone tells you to stand & the world
decides for a time to listen. That little girl

inside the woman inside the bus releases
one impossibly red balloon. The string

a goodbye. A final goodbye. Where once
bodies, names. Where once skin, texture,

amalgam, that heart-shaped ascension
our mothers promised, in their lucid moments,

would come with a little faith. Pulled from
the bus, handcuffed & unforgiven, the girl

still thrashing inside smiles. Smiles. Tomorrow
these streets will run red with unrequited love.

INVASIVE

Then there was no more singing.
All the lights in their throats cut:

the protest of evening wolves & black
bears nuzzling a parched creek for any-

thing that might sustain them another
white-skinned winter, those foreign

birds we never learned the names for.
Invasive, my grandfather called them.

Like the silver carp haunting our
local river. Bullfrogs & possums.

He called us *natives* after living
three generations on the same

hard land it took so much blood
to own. At the end of the path

the bullet takes to meet the right
body, the right body drops like

nothing worth losing sleep over.
It'll cost two men three hours

to drag it home in one piece.
That wilder silence lasts but

a brief eternity. Before the unseen
choir shakes the forest. Again,

the same damn wolves & starlings. Men
still dragging. The season closing.

Its wiry legs kick & quiver in our hands.
Like strings. Song. Our song now to sing.

ARMISTICE

You could tell from the start these stars

weren't the right kind of candles & night
not wounded enough to call it an altar;

just a few pale scars where a violence
that once held things together went all
peaceful & loose & downwind from
yesterday's bodies a terrible absence of rot.

The birds weren't saying *secession*
or *internment* anymore. The churches
weren't burning or singing the rafters
clear of mice. The old hanging tree

out back shook free its histories, roots
nourished by a silent rain. The boys
who normally would be numbers by now
dismantled their oaths & fathers never lifted

their shotguns from the mantle; the animals
allowed to eat each other again, to scavenge
& wail & find their own places to die, ungently.
Nowhere a daughter fenced off from a mother

who hauled her gods over miles of unbroken desert
to finally say *home*. Then have even this taken away.
Yes, this was a river meant for crossing.
This was just another dream

in a landscape flush with unbreakable dreams
of a river that could be crossed without bridge,

without sacrificing a single star to the current.

ASSIMILATION

As immigrant stars bundle into constellations for warmth, security.

As the cargo hold of a great ship wails & in one voice prays
        toward another country.

Interned by hope, how a body burns brighter when it has something
        to hold fast to.

Horizon // fresh flag // just a single memory of your daughter
        before the pinning down
& breaking in, laughs passing between soldiers like cigarettes
        or ripe dates.

If it's true we're all cross-examined by the same light, why
        are my son & daughter
sleeping uninjured beneath white waves of cotton & candle?
        The moon above unarmed.

The least lit star enough to guide us home. As we're not learning
the language of the world so much as giving it familiar names.

A vowel here. A mother's god there. Accent dropped. Innocence repaired
for yet another round of restless men.

THE MOON IS TWO HALF-MOONS JOINED TOGETHER

Her body still // yoked to histories retold // so often even her great-grandmother, who lived it, cannot // remember the river's name she // crossed to get here. *Tigris. Rio Grande. Euphrates.* How the men & more // men & when the men were done, they'd touch finger to forehead to chest to shoulder & zip up their flies. How sometimes the world // works like that. The bullet passes right // through & on the other side another // language to learn, another god to // feed, & a child that wears half your face. *Try not to take it // as a sign, how they see // you*, momma says. The books the kids don't read don't mention it. *This* name. That *first* name. The constellations it takes to turn // sky into map. How boys still // rock-paper-scissor their way to cruelty, which hurts // less than their taking her // as white, which at least means they love // what they see. & a red clay stain that once was a river.

THAT IS REALLY JUST ROPE

Elsewhere, wrapped in scars,
a dirt road broadens to highway:

winter keeps its bones well-hidden
under a great white weight:

the goldfinches a child frees from
her mouth return uneaten by larger

birds. We fall hard for these things.
A promise of deep green blades

pushing up through concrete. A sky
this lit without need for gasoline

& matches & restlessness. Grief
that is really just a healed-over

history. Elsewhere, hanging from
the same branches, bodiless, rope—

MY AMERICAN GHOST

so draw the eyelids
            shut & forget the fire
tangled among the branches
of your spine
                —Michael Wasson

& we shall be lit

    like the dark haloes

clay pigeons stain onto a lawn

    before shattering: how sun-

light strikes a coin

    differently after a train

flattens its face: another furious

    daybreak lost behind clouds.

& our mouths, nestfuls of promises,

    we shall open them almost

fully: swallow & speak for what

    we've swallowed: a whole

new language of witness. Shadows

mean there's something up there

lighting us from behind, right? Breaking means

some of us are still intact. Let's

follow the Rorschach of blackbirds

with our crosshairs & choose

not to fire, or fire & own it. I confess

I don't think we're ready

just yet to own our ghosts.

NO
GOOD
NIGHT

INCENDIARY DEVICE

The thought of all this country burning
beyond bright: unearthly colors buried

deep in the earth, released, incite the oak
to awe. Is it true this ruin has been ours

the whole time? The generations spent
praying to the heavens for a match tip,

the demons exorcised, returning every
evening in the familiar form of a father's

fist. The fire is a blanket pulled over
the field, up to its eyes, to hide the monsters

imagined in our closet. Or to expose them
for what they are. The animals have

always been terrified of us. They know
something of love we admit only to night.

It turns out I was born with a matchbook
in my hands. I don't need to reach out or up.

O the thought of this country, all these
homes dancing sparks into a hot & holy

starless sky. There's a reason we refuse
to leave, even now. Is it true, father,

when the world finally says its name
it will be in our voice?

DARK TOURIST

I wouldn't say it's the bodies
implied by unmarked mounds
of looted earth or these rituals
meant to keep the dead
precious & silent as a mother
once her children are all raised
up or vanished. It's not the stray
hairs goldened by age anchored to
a skull, still catching & holding
the light like a fist. All these living
war zones. The twenty evacuated
kilometers of fallout. The abnormal
concentration of history in a single
rice patty. The hands that continue
to work it. The dead-eyed oxen.
My being moved, finally. There is
a small chapel in Czech exquisitely
adorned in 70,000 skeletons no matter
how hard I hold my mother's thinning
hand I cannot unsee. It's when I tell her
I can still love her like this. Breathless,
material, pillaged. Then moving on.

THE SACRED

Someone is cramming notes into a wall
she knows no one   will ever read.

Someone is banging her head into a wall

                    as prayer

which works for a time.
                    All the sacred

openings of her body have been filled
so often by men without the necessary

                        permissions

borders don't mean   *keep out*   anymore

    & there is no such thing as *stay*

                        safely inside.

Someone is plugging up the holes in the wall
with starlings her son strangled with his bare hands.

That there is no father is a blessing. Blessed,

what she once called *my light* is turning into
                    such a fine boy.

All around her,
waves of holy people wash in & out, wail & wail
then walk sixteen miles home for rice & fish.

Someone's heart is quiet   as a prison yard.
Someone has more paper than prayers. Light

          suffers through the cracks in the wall,
          ricochets off into the city, then sand.

She pulls another bird from her box of dead birds.

SEPARATIONS

Silver wires partition bodies
from the bodies they birthed
six years ago in wire-thin
stucco houses open-walled
to dust & sky. An infinite
backdrop of silent scars
& in the foreground little
changes of the uniforms
but the faces pushing up
from them like sunflowers
uncertain which way
the wind wants them
to sway. A migraine of
cameras stalks the well-lit
edges. Wash basins over-
flow with tears. Another
appealed-to horizon burns
with forsaken promises.
                    It's true:
we've always run toward
the wrong light. Always
a somewhere that hurts
less than home. Families
subdivide until there is
nothing left but memory
& wail & holding that wail
up to their ears like song
& singing it. Singing it.

UNCOORDINATED EFFORTS

"Desperation set in": Puerto Ricans grab shovels, machetes to help restore power
—CBS News; February 7, 2018

Sometimes a palmful of water is enough
to keep an island from statehood, power.

Sometimes it takes shovels & machetes
to carve one's name in the same earth

that yields so willingly to others. Human
currency devalues quicker than paper.

A raft rolling wildly—sometimes spilling
its children into the surf, sometimes even

reaching us intact—can always be turned
away. & home can be made as strenuous

as passage. That we are not them helps
restore our faith in ourselves. We watch

poles hoist skyward in prayer—lines sparking,
alive in communication—& know some good

can come of suffering. That's the Jesus we hold
up for worship. That's the West we praise

our great-grandparents for taming for us.
Sometimes another's grit gives a people

back its power, sometimes even their vote. Still,
unbordered doesn't always imply incorporated.

Or empathy, aide. It's a wonder we can even see them through
all the seabirds lining up to roost on their unbroken backs.

CÉSAR ESTRADA CHÁVEZ // ROBERT FROST

Where two roads diverge, an orchard
rests its throat in migrant hands: body
reaching into another body: beautifully

raw sustenance exhumed: each pinch
of green a prayer to distant family: every
goddamn callus a reason not to go gentle.

// I have been one acquainted with the night. //

Now a makeshift trailer meant to keep the world
in its place keeps the men & women under-
paid & unable to taste an unowned world: this

choreographed violence: bloodless revolution:
coerced hunger replaced by chosen, regardless: huddled
masses: crucible of root & sky: to look up and see, still,

// there is no good night. //

THE LAST SUNSET

never mind the men who roam that myth /
horseback, fly-sheathed, defined by the lands
left to conquer, dirty / in the way of unmarried
pregnant women, how at the end of each rope
a body / all the wood it takes to make a cross
out of air / the part our grandfathers played in
breaking in the West // mind instead the sunset
forever splayed behind them, the *moving into*
before they called it *progress* / how all it takes
is a single star to read the sky // roughly drawn
paradise, without an altar

PROTOTYPE

Another smoke-gorged sky
erases the diorama carefully
constructed of matchsticks
cut felt broken oaths what
older folks call *history* my son
is learning other words for
lashed & stretched over a
cardboard shoebox leather
strips that once meant mountain
that once cradled coal & gods
& white-tailed deer like someone
else's mother like little rosaries
green plastic men arraign into
settler & savage & everything
has faith enough to burn all
these child-hands upending
entire wagon trains setting
the steepled horizon ablaze
dozens of impossible families
melt into sawdust standing in
for prairie standing in for *more
home please* the whole damn
thing a mess of lost landscapes
ancestors teachers furiously
breaking down tables unspooling
hoses flooding the papered valley
leaving us something vaguely
true to bring home as proof of

THE DROWNING HOUSE

The rain is a hood   pulled over the world.
Our neighbor's house, vanishes.   & its windows
through which we watch things   undress.
The plastic deer neck-bent   as if chewing up the lawn
go the way of other deer,   of the wolves,   the arroyo
turned creek again.   & beyond that somewhere
we pass through as quickly as our pickup allows   a dry reservation.

Sightless, *driven*   more than driving, we leave   briefly
       for that higher ground.

       & in our absence,
if our cellar floods, well,   it'll give us a reason
for bucket & heft. If the slot machines mommy pumps her grocery store
checks into makes the water there more   potable, a reason.
If my brother picks another fight with someone who's name isn't
quite like ours. If the horses   goddamn everywhere recognize
the yoke of our hands. If from these hills
       I can witness

our home, consuming & being   consumed. The ironwood
    I knifed my name   into wash itself clean.   The deer return.
    If the deer return   daddy says   wolves won't be far behind.
    Shotgun & fences. I can't see our fence   from here.
The barbs, what catches on them.   The valley floor. It's wide-open
mouths we fill with English.

SECOND GENERATION

That we can drop like lost airplanes & strike
towers eight minutes apart. That we can trace
our mother's maiden name back to a country
we can hardly pronounce. The sins of others
reflected in our faces like moonlight caught
in the face of a shovel. I don't know much
about physics, but I'm pretty sure some things
fall faster than others. Like accents when a country
demands one tongue. Like bodies inconsistently
colored. The light takes so long to leak through
morning clouds sometimes I wonder if I should
still call this night. That real night, the one star-
broken & flagless that we remember so vividly
though we've never seen it, with its brilliant
freedoms making predators of us all.

FIGUREHEAD

Lashed & anchored to the front of each ship,
a woman—breasts carved from dark oak,
all the wildness sanded down, polished out;
half human, half fish, a grotesque fantasy
every boy raised within earshot of an ocean
has touched himself under the covers of night
envisioning in bed beside him. How we love
running our hands along the bow of another's
impossible body. When no one is looking,
how even the old sailors who've broken
& been broken by flesh & blood women
weep at this promise, unfulfilled. Opening
one to the next, whitecaps pour secrets into
& steal those same secrets from each other.
Ashen clouds collect themselves into storm.
It's too easy to lament we've wasted our lives.
The women we've made to withstand us
withstand us.

SEED

who do not want to be mothers / whose bodies
pinned starless against a soft green midnight
field, no longer their own / who want for little
more than / that fenced-in barbed wire tongue
boys speak with / behind the shuttered liquor
shop among disassembled machinery, mostly
car parts & dog howls / silos penitently bent,
graceless, pleading for it, for grace / whose
mothers gave them names knowing nothing
lasts high school / except this / & the silence,
the ruin / who names it

PICTURE DAY

Now let's see
that shuttered motel

behind your eyes.
Vacancy still pulsing

neon red into night.
Absolute night. Yes,

the kind that hurts
like a dragged cross,

like the promise
a country you have

traveled so far to
love rescinds.

Now hold that pose,
your chin so heavy

it ruptures your chest.
Carry the empty

weight of words
creased in your brow.

Follow the light of this
new dawn down

the barrel of a gun.
Any wound will do

as long as you keep it
open. Remember

where you come from
& the dead in your lungs.

Like rail tracks made
obsolete by a highway,

thistle & crabgrass
overcoming a field.

Like a bell with no rope
to ring it. Yes, smile

just like that. Say this
is now your home.

CONQUISTADOR

That with intent—pure
as any born of subjugation & erasure; christened

holy by those who've spent their lives
defining it for others—to make cathedrals of

their bodies, if not their souls (should they have them,
like beasts worshipped for their sustenance who may yet hold

certain keys to certain unopenable doors).
There is no metaphor for loving the world so hard

it falls freely on your sword, gives its entirety
to your gods. There is no saving, only offering.

×

When that fire enters, each bone unburnt
is a failure, a reason to love fiercer—no mild graces

ever expanded an empire inward. Inward the breath
the children hold to play dead. To play

dead, the children nestle
back into their mothers'

bodies, already draining of their heavens. That *they didn't know
the path until shown*—glorious, gold-rimmed & relentless

as a born-into slavery. A worn-in field. Toppled altar. Becoming
human, finally, in yoke & hallelujah.

SISYPHUS // ROGER AILES

In this story the boulder hurts him less
pouring back down that steep hill.

It's the village below that flattens;
mothers that look nothing like his

or the women he consumed flood
a Texas *family detention facility*;

their children learn how to settle
into cruelty, the crouch and crush

of anonymity; a whiplash of torches
casket an otherwise pleasant white

anytown main street; an unquiet
border wall divides in- from exhale.

The smile Camus paints on his rock-
soft face refuses to surrender to gravity,

joyously. *Halleluiah, inconsequential*
aftermaths. Praise collateral damage.

That there is nothing apart from the push
some still call prayer. Heart. Heroism.

That this aped anthem just keeps singing
itself hungry. That no matter how brutal

a king, the narrative the gods fashioned
for him from *another's* human clay

daggers its way into my father's living
room every night. As we eat what someone

else killed. As he tries to tuck my children into
a myth that calcifies the louder he conjures it.

I TEND TO SEE LOVE AS AN ABSENCE OF CONTEXT

Earlier, the sky. The unchurched pigeons holding the sky up by its steeple. Stars made of blown glass blowing off this lip of sky as if the earth's as flat as Homer envisioned. *Oceanus.* Or any encircling body. Earlier, a mother. A hand-me-down heaven tattered as any blanket meant to swaddle an entire life. A life still in conversation with that gone body. Earlier, to make loss holy, they called it *providence.* Now we tend to let the ashes scatter. To make room for whatever comes next, we shoo the pigeons from the steeple holding up the sky & let things fall where they must. Shattered glass underfoot. I guess now we call it gravity. Earlier—

DISSOLVE

That there were children here once
(calling these neon plains   home
carving the men they dreamed of

becoming into cedar) & men   (dissolving
moon-like into myth while their bodies continued
panning the dried-out riverbeds for lost   wildness)

& mothers (braiding light through their daughters' hair)
& believe it or not animals (goddamn everywhere) clustered
together for warmth   taking winter deep in-

to their lungs & giving back plume   childbearing
hills   untapped oil reservoired beneath them   more stars
than a nation could excise in a century   a sky deprived

of its knives   That there are now utility roads
bearing their names that snake along the pipeline   That we take
these roads   That   regardless   we keep taking these roads

BLOOM

— for Kazim Ali

Yesterday it was leaves, now snow
suffocates the seeds. What's meant

to flower flowers underground or
not at all or we haven't the kind

of eyes that recognize color breaking
earth, skyward, toward us, our feet —

×

which have always been another word
for crush, which is how we get to know

×

greening things. But any wound will do.
Really, any weather can hurt or be hurt

by our raised & restless hands. A sudden light
razors down from the heavens & strikes

like a father's fist an unempty field.
One then another tree sparks & smolders.

Seeds displace. Seeds refuse to displace.
Because we too were planted offseason,

×

my father says, as if to calm the dead
& dying seeds inside me. Go ahead,

let things see your brief bloom, your wilting.
Say this world is worth its trembling.

SUMMON

SELF-PORTRAIT AS LACUNA

What do we do with a body
        severed from other bodies,

with a child who cannot weave herself
        into & out of embrace?

When the plastic stars glued to her ceiling
        supplant the celestial, dreams

& hungers cast only so high, prayers smacked
        hard against drywall & blue paint?

Into the burn barrel out back, everything I hoped
        would someday wear her name. Family,

only a state away, already dimming to memory. Only
        my face to remind her of her own.

A miniature dollhouse world, prematurely on fire. This
        afflicted air. Breath. When breathing

becomes the barbed fence between neighbors.
        Cover yourself, love. Please.

It is my splintered cross to keep you safely distanced
        from humanity. Here, another promise

I didn't mean to break. Here, another kiss as apology.
        A board book to show what it was like

before. Talking animals to prove the world can be
        wildly unquiet. & innocent. A sky

made up of myths. & stars. Honest-to-goodness stars.
    All gas & flame & unobstructed whimsy.

Here is someone else's tree to carve your initials into.
    Here, love, is the tree of my body

to learn to climb. Far from here. From me. To touch
    whatever's still up there, beautifully above us.

NIKOLA TESLA // MALALA YOUSAFZAI

> — *if your hate could be turned into electricity, it would light up the whole world*

Lend me a new god   (of kindle & current; boldly   broken vessel)
to pray to tonight. Tonight the earth   thunderheads & overhead
an absence of anchor. When the half of me not feigning   sleep
unwinds & unprivileges,   your starsong hurts   as it should
have always hurt. All bodies   a conduit   for other bodies. (Less
ocean between us now   for bullets to bridge.) Lend me that love
letter drilled into your skull.   Please   forgive my disbelief in
impossible things.   When they came for you,   a girl was born
in a boat looking up   at a now-navigable night sky.   No one left
to drown her compass.   No body left   to steal that spark.
Please lend me your (recklessly simple)   song. Your wireless
tower, cascading heavens.   A textbook. Just one unruined
schoolhouse. The world   (until there's no one left to sing it).

—for Kelly Grace Thomas

FIRST OCEAN

Before [we] close
our eyes to see
what night asks [us]
to let go
            —Craig Santos Perez

Wondrous, not yet
polluted by *beauty* // the skeletal

shipwrecks as men [we'll] hang our children from
by the wrists in photos to prove something

about lineage today swim

the shallows making nests for fish // before vow
-wels & consonants break *seeing* apart like rice in water //

before undertows, *deprived of,* all that longing for
a return to the impossible // before believing

with our hands steepled over cold
bodies already shedding their names // this is

the story [we'll] forget; this is //

a story [we'll] remember nooseless, hyphenated only by seabirds //

before the anchor's hesitation, an overcast of doubt
-ful clouds // before [we] learn to call it prayer: this

loving //

sprigs of early morning light reach down to us
without pricking: *hurt* // [we] walk into the sea //

into what we don't yet know is a sea // strapped
to our mothers' chests // unbalanced, shivering, *alive*

SELF-PORTRAIT OF PUBLIC CRUCIFIXION

Sanded down edges, splinters shorn, nothing
for skin to catch on but the nails driven deep

into night by a man who looks, as always,
too much like my father. He knifes his name

into the soft cedar beneath the feet of someone
else's savior. Then a heart. A love note, perhaps,

to an unlived childhood. That wounded sunset
that hangs between lovers' initials. Before all

that manhood takes hold. Before the rope
swinging in rural shade loses its tire & becomes

something else entirely. All their broken-lashed
windows thrown open, our neighbors are hungry.

We're all hungry. The pies cooling on the sill aren't enough.
Whatever it takes to bless a body back to innocence,

we want to witness. Our children must endure.
Through the tiny gaps in tiny clenched fingers,

the only world we can offer sits Catholically
calm. The cross hurts less than it should. Night

hurts less. A man who isn't quite my father stretches
the next body over the next slice of cedar. Sands down

the stars. Shears. Smooths. Lovingly lays his hand on
a hammer. Raises. Rising overhead, thrushes scatter into song.

INCARNATE

Balm: as in a handsaw taken
to dying branches; my mother

when she prayed us cut the air
off, those final gasps the purest

she'd ever known; as in that time
the doe the dogs left living by a thread

leaned that thread into our bullet;
as in the unnamed herbs my wife's

grandmother swears held her head
sweaty & adolescent, but upright,

astral, cradled by the only kind of arms
the internment camp had to offer, that

child-size tea set she smuggled through
a half-century's worth of indignities

that now rests on our mantle, chipped
from our own children's violent whims,

themselves the balm, those missing
wedges, those unspoken memories;

as in the aged neighbor who just handed
me two rolls of toilet paper because loss

means something different when the whole
boat is sinking; as in my gratitude, my selfish

gratitude for everything I haven't had to steal,
the shreds of light that makes this loving less a cage.

JEAN-MICHEL BASQUIAT // HARRIET TUBMAN

"When I found I had crossed that line, I looked at my hands to see if I was the same person."
—H. T.

Burn barrel. Cuffed, hungry hands. Morning twilight.
& with a bit of paint, newsprint can be repurposed into

something truer. My dead, for example. How theirs is
history while another's is *myth*. A tall tale handed down

generations over makeshift fires of a woman who could not
read or write freeing words from their reins. Breathe,

language. Remind me how breath can be a luxury. It takes
time for a genuflected knee to suffocate the sky. *Sky, words,*

morning, bodies roughly sketched onto a concrete canvas.
A few wear their crowns like halos. Mouths a permanent

scar. Teeth jagged. Bared. & all those impossible colors
contrasted into accuracy. Personhood. In a certain light,

how everything is self-portrait. How they called her Moses.
How white the Moses over my grandfather's well-lit mantle.

Do you tire, young man, of shouldering so much nothing? Nothing
but 300 hearts smuggled north. 300 names. Given names. *Master*

names. Graffiti. High art. A bronze statue, as apology. Celebration.
They're gonna kill me. I cannot breathe bejeweled onto the base.

MASK

By then, it's assumed,
though not certain, the faces cradled within, less like an infant every
    chest-trembling cough,
are *enemy, other*. Not the kind of *pitied* that snakes every so often into
    compassion for, not

                    the shadow that defines the light it angles,
more—I'm seeing clearly now for the first time, terrified as I am for my
    son's frequently shallow
breaths—the rage of snow at spring's gentle fingers, that unholy green
    penetration of meadow

              grass; how it is *vulnerable* turns us *monstrous*; the barn
out back sill in conversation with its burning, even now, after all these
    years rebuilding
from foundation up—to roof, to firmament, heavens? —there is some-
    thing to hold:

      not *onto*, exactly, maybe *out for*,
as in *let me hold you, son, out for the wolves*, as if it's fair to call them
    wolves, these
masked women cradling their own children like stars—not stars, exact-
    ly—eyeing the cloth

    I sing through. Nowadays, these gloves I use to touch.

CHARCOAL NUDE

Roughed-up: edges   indistinct: body
softly black & blending with all this white
            space. The paper:

less a canvas than a mirror.   That she is displayed here at all
is a minor miracle, the kind the old folks call
            assimilation.

      Not pictured:

the artist: his intent: that half-moon smile
when the legs are complete   & the infinite
            opening between.

Weaponized beauty, that we are meant to   touch
ourselves with suspicion. Or is it guilt? A sordid history erased
        or on full display, depending on

the context. The framed notecard doesn't give us

            her name.

COUNTERGLOW

Consider the meteorite,
   110,000 pounds of

debris that hollowed out
   Wolfe Creek Crater;

how Oppenheimer's boldest
   nightmares couldn't

concoct the kind of ruin
   that vanishes a sky

for years; how anything can
   become a tourist attraction.

Consider what we do to ourselves
   when the one person we love

renounces our touch. Consider angels,
   my grandmother used to say,

& how you never know which saves
   & which consumes us; whatever

you believe, how it all comes down
   to flame. There's too much

written about the end. Pale horses &
   rogue nukes & the smaller gods

of razor & lukewarm bathwater. When I
   consider each meal is someone's

last, am I meant to lose my appetite
　　or keep dragging my fork

over this emptied plate, never sated?
　　Consider how we become our own

conclusion; how what we've hung out
　　to dry remains crucified; how believing

these things beautiful might not make them so.
　　Consider how rivers multiply

into ocean; a few misplaced words & now
　　the bombs have their wings.

& so much goddamn waiting, as if we have to
　　imagine what nooses do to necks.

Consider what's been redacted from life
　　to make all this anguish seem an art.

IT'S NOT CORPSES WE BURN ON PYRES ANYMORE

Or witches, pleading to whatever gods it took
to raise one nation from the living embers of another.

Or *holy* men. Or *dirty* women. The body scraps
even scavengers won't drag deeper into night.

In hindsight our heroes weren't so much
the *saving from* kind. Conquistadors & secret

slave owners. Gunslingers. Lovers hard & wild
as the lands they tamed. Great-grandfathers.

Sometimes America breaks our hearts
& sometimes we'd kill for a chance

to do the breaking. There are no plagues
anymore. No carnations or camphor, masks

overflowing with healing spices. No
rickety carts shopping for the dead.

No need to paint a red cross on our door.
& someone's cut all the ropes from the trees.

America, let's just walk these suburban streets
together, hand in hand, in love with nothing

we have to put much love into. Pull from
my mouth a different animal, one without

teeth or howl. Let's just stack our homes
into a pyre our ancestors would be proud of.

Let it scrape the sky raw. Like prayer. Babel.
Then leave it unlit.

THE WOLVES HAVE DONE THEIR WORST

& then they say things like
all the good days are behind us

& if both can be true, I don't know what
to promise my children over their monster-broken sleep about tomorrow.

When they ask to crawl back inside their mother
because the cardboard airplanes circling their cribs might crash

into the thin glass buildings of their bodies,

when they notice how my scrapes & bruises don't heal
so easily anymore, when the anchorwoman prophesizes rain & more rain
& if

there is any more rain the river will swallow the house
for good this time;

when they are old enough to wear my face as a mask & then a country's
& then
when there are no more masks to wear they will say these same things
over the same

cradles beneath the hijacked flightpaths of the same poorly-
painted paper planes; if only both can be true—loving & wanting

the world to end before the wolves
show themselves beneath my tongue, & theirs.

I TOO TAKE SHELTER IN THE BODY,

in the picks & plows, millstones, the indelicate hands working
a country back into loose soil. Above me, the once-scattered stars

clump together for warmth. Only so much remains for my daughter
to wish upon, for my son to name after mythical beasts, for my father

to cradle between steepled fingers reciting my mother's name over
& over into specter. & our branches tire from holding so much

nothing. Rope swing snapped, not anything like a noose. Wild grass
browning around an empty silo. Not at all like the torch-lit bodies

the papers promise will wash away with the next good rain. I too
take shelter in this Catholic silence, in the overworked machinery rusted

in place, reddening the field, in these patchwork hands whiter than
next season's hard frost. Here, a burn barrel for our unmended shingles,

the collapsed shed out back, the part of the animal we didn't bother to eat. Here,
son, is your myth, your beast, where we watch a fawn crawl back into bullet.

MEADOWSLASH

Gun-pop, bird-scatter, barely a body

left but the one the dog drags obediently back to the house
      as if mastering one thing makes him
            sovereign.

    We don't have the heart

    to tell him the rest of the country's on fire
    & there's not a damn thing we can do
    but rush him out into the brush again
            demanding offerings.

    It's simpler this way. Each his own god
            paying tribute to those who whip
            & nourish him. Home

    as a paperweight. Around our edges, grasses wild & bend,

            so close

            to blowing away. Heaven

as a nest of castoffs, a table to feed under, bone & gristle, a hand
    to nuzzle, a buckshot of birds
            fleeing yet another brief sanctum.

POSTSCRIPT FOR A FLYOVER COUNTRY

so too the bruises   the outlived machinery   every empty rain-
rusted silo scorching   the skyline praying   grains rise all Jesus-
like to refill its mouth & as if all water is walkable how little we
really know of the bridgeless river   our dead *civilizing* & spreading
seed & here we are crossing over   recalling a primary school montage
of covered wagons loaded to the teeth with popsicle stick figures bent
over burlap-sewn oxen   a few flecks of paint for blood   the same
water now 34,000 feet below & arid   as a memory withheld   because
it hurts less than it should because there's an order in which things are broken
because i carry my grandfather's rags & rages   like a cross that isn't really
anything like a cross   to make room for yet another bridge another sky-
line raw & hungry broken-down body   combine plowshare boyhood
another cow leans into its bolt   foreclosed heaven   somewhere
down there   home, its windows kicked in

SUMMON

Say: a pit bull unchained from a tree
is no more vicious than everything

else we've eventually cut free from it.
Tire swing. Beer cans & our sisters'

dolls bitten by air rifles. The bodies
we call an erasable half of a history.

Say: noose. Say: light turns to halo
when cast through the empty eye of rope.

After centuries of playing at manhood, say:
the borders have softened. Say: we are not

only our father's fathers anymore; hell,
we cannot stop ourselves from saying it.

But this new burning is the same burning
is a cross lighting the lawn of a vacant church

is an apology in past tense is how we unbind
the dolls from that unbreakable branch & hand them

back to a little sister who says it's okay the holes
we've shot into; I'll get used to how the wind whistles through.

A POEM IN WHICH EVERYONE SURVIVES UNTIL DAWN

As in the hard heart // of an avocado, the part we cut
around, // amputate, curse // when what's left isn't enough

to sate our hunger. As in that // beautiful roadside bouquet
bound to a guardrail // meant to celebrate loss, to warn us

children // still live here. How // the light angled
through this angel // oak, on certain clear // mornings,

appears as a noose. As in // that history. As in // a rewritten
history. My ancestors now // nowhere in it. // As in the distances

grandad's eyes fled // to find himself // forgiven, all that
burnt acreage between us // a fistful of water // could smother

if unclenched into palm. // Touch. Please. // How my son looks at me
that way. // Still. // That ugly cathedral I didn't mean to build // beneath

his tongue. That bridge in trying // not to collapse I've kicked
the beams from. Bridge, as in // a temporary crossing. // River,

as in always // somehow crossable. Despite us. // Sturdy, as in persistent,
as in // I'm sorry, son, as in I pray // the world refuses // to rust you entirely.

EVERYTHING HERE IS BEAUTIFUL

& full of thrum. You can tell by how far

a lie must travel down string into paper cup to reach the ear as true.

How we recognize a starling best when its song is absent.

How everything that comes to rest eventually comes to rest

in precisely the right place.

A boy buried beneath the rubble of a blown-up building can tell you

the sky—suffocated & leaden, leading nowhere —

has horded all its light just for him.

A gut-shot doe will drag its limp limbs miles to a particular pinyon's shade.

Maybe everything is just too damn close;

from very far away

how the massive mountains shadowing the town & the town

& our bodies equally slight.

HARPS STRUNG WITH GUT STILL MAKE MUSIC AFTER 2,000 YEARS[1]

Twelve unpaired shoes hang
          windless from a wire

      threading streetlights together. Eventually
swallows reclaim them. Without the need

for twig & try, raise a family in our cavities. My son
         points a toy gun to my temple;

each *bang* reminds me my father was once a mountain
            that crumbled

beneath me — how the sheer terror of cradling
         so much weightlessness

      can flatten landscapes, raze cities,
or, the birds remind me, return warmth to discarded

things. That there is nothing that is not home
         hurts

more than the imagined bullet drilling into my skull.
      I cannot fail to forgive it.

As he tightens his tiny lips and blows
         through me, finally,

I am song.

---

1. A line from the poem "Future Self" by Diana Khoi Nguyen (*Ghost of*, Omnidawn, 2018)

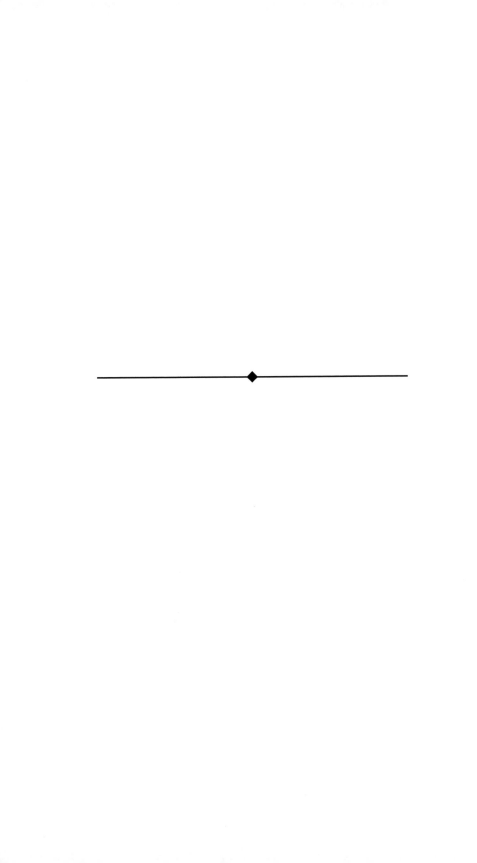

MY HEART IS IN THE MOUTH OF ANOTHER HEART

May the deer navigate   this field of white crosses
         & tiny windless flags

as if no one buried beneath has ever taken from them.

May we join the mice nesting   in our bones
            like rotten logs

       & raise our children safely shadowed
                         in grief.

May the children we've chosen for sacrifice climb
so high in these elms the light   that rarely reaches us

     trembles at their coming.

     Trembles & comes to them.

Someday the need to sing will become the song
         & the song grow into another need.

   Not for blood this time. Not oil. Otherness.

Among the burning crosses, churches, refineries at dusk, a bridge
that shouldn't be there. May we say we see it through the smoke.

       Like forgiveness. All this impossible forgiveness.

May the dead believe us when we say it.

John Sibley Williams is the author of seven poetry collections, including *Scale Model of a Country at Dawn* (Cider Press Review Poetry Award), *The Drowning House* (Elixir Press Poetry Award), *As One Fire Consumes Another* (Orison Poetry Prize), *Skin Memory* (Backwaters Prize, University of Nebraska Press), and *Summon* (JuxtaProse Chapbook Prize). A twenty-six-time Pushcart nominee, John is the winner of numerous awards, including the Wabash Prize for Poetry, Philip Booth Award, Phyllis Smart-Young Prize, and Laux/Millar Prize. He serves as editor of *The Inflectionist Review* and founder of the Caesura Poetry Workshop series. Previous publishing credits include *Best American Poetry, Yale Review, Verse Daily, North American Review, Prairie Schooner,* and *TriQuarterly.*

ELIXIR PRESS TITLES

Poetry

Circassian Girl by Michelle Mitchell-Foust

Imago Mundi by Michelle Mitchell-Foust

Distance From Birth by Tracy Philpot

Original White Animals by Tracy Philpot

Flow Blue by Sarah Kennedy

A Witch's Dictionary by Sarah Kennedy

The Gold Thread by Sarah Kennedy

Rapture by Sarah Kennedy

Monster Zero by Jay Snodgrass

Drag by Duriel E. Harris

Running the Voodoo Down by Jim McGarrah

Assignation at Vanishing Point by Jane Satterfield

Her Familiars by Jane Satterfield

The Jewish Fake Book by Sima Rabinowitz

Recital by Samn Stockwell

Murder Ballads by Jake Adam York

Floating Girl (Angel of War) by Robert Randolph

Puritan Spectacle by Robert Strong

X-testaments by Karen Zealand

Keeping the Tigers Behind Us by Glenn J. Freeman

Bonneville by Jenny Mueller

State Park by Jenny Mueller

Cities of Flesh and the Dead by Diann Blakely

Green Ink Wings by Sherre Myers

Orange Reminds You Of Listening by Kristin Abraham

In What I Have Done & What I Have Failed To Do by Joseph P. Wood

Bray by Paul Gibbons

The Halo Rule by Teresa Leo

Perpetual Care by Katie Cappello

The Raindrop's Gospel: The Trials of St. Jerome and St. Paula by Maurya Simon

Prelude to Air from Water by Sandy Florian

Let Me Open You A Swan by Deborah Bogen

Cargo by Kristin Kelly

Spit by Esther Lee

Rag & Bone by Kathryn Nuerenberger

Kingdom of Throat-stuck Luck by George Kalamaras

Mormon Boy by Seth Brady Tucker

Nostalgia for the Criminal Past by Kathleen Winter

I will not kick my friends by Kathleen Winter

Little Oblivion by Susan Allspaw

Quelled Communiqués by Chloe Joan Lopez

Stupor by David Ray Vance

Curio by John A. Nieves

The Rub by Ariana-Sophia Kartsonis

Visiting Indira Gandhi's Palmist by Kirun Kapur

Freaked by Liz Robbins

Looming by Jennifer Franklin

Flammable Matter by Jacob Victorine

Prayer Book of the Anxious by Josephine Yu

flicker by Lisa Bickmore

Sure Extinction by John Estes

Selected Proverbs by Michael Cryer

Rise and Fall of the Lesser Sun Gods by Bruce Bond

Barnburner by Erin Hoover

Live from the Mood Board by Candice Reffe

Deed by Justin Wymer

Somewhere to Go by Laurin Becker Macios

If We Had a Lemon We'd Throw It and Call That the Sun by Christopher Citro

White Chick by Nancy Keating

The Drowning House by John Sibley Williams

Fiction

How Things Break by Kerala Goodkin

Juju by Judy Moffat

Grass by Sean Aden Lovelace

Hymn of Ash by George Looney

The Worst May Be Over by George Looney

Nine Ten Again by Phil Condon

Memory Sickness by Phong Nguyen

Troglodyte by Tracy DeBrincat

The Loss of All Lost Things by Amina Gautier

The Killer's Dog by Gary Fincke

Everyone Was There by Anthony Varallo

The Wolf Tone by Christy Stillwell

Tell Me, Signora by Ann Harleman

Far West by Ron Tanner